Time to Take Us Back

Time to Take Us Back
A Poetry Collection

Kelly Carter Schneider

Kelly Schneider Writes
St. Louis, Missouri

Copyright © 2025 Kelly Carter Schneider. All rights reserved.

No part of this publication may be reproduced, distributed, or transmitted in any form or by any means, including photocopying, recording, or other electronic or mechanical methods, without the prior written permission of the publisher, except as permitted by U.S. copyright law. For permission requests, contact KellyCarterSchneider@gmail.com.

ISBN: 979-8-9919752-0-9
Library of Congress Control Number: 2024924148
Printed in the United States of America.

Cover photo: Kelly Carter Schneider
Cover design: Hannah Battista
Book design by Peggy Nehmen: n-kcreative.com

Published by Kelly Schneider Writes
kellyschneiderwrites.com

BISAC: POETRY / Women Authors
POETRY / Subjects & Themes / Family

In memory of
my friend,
Tom Isbell

The Monarch doesn't wonder who she is,
Or where she's going;
Ripening in the dark,
Or flowering in the light.

Like milkweed grows,
Manifesting The Way,
Unfolding her wings,
She just does.

—**Tom Isbell**

CONTENTS

Author's Note 1

Part One

Tom's Gone 7
Daddy's Hand 13
Weekend Fun 15
Chewing Gum and Duct Tape 19
Lindsey's Birth 23
Lucky Ladies 25
Work Snack 27
Abby Rae's Birth 29
Forgotten Town 31
Dream Walker 35
Jack's Birth 37

Part Two

The D-Word 41
Dream Retreat: A Bad Rap 43
Third Time's a Charm: An Anniversary Poem 47
A Mother's Worry 49
Mundane Moments 51
The Test of Time 55
Pop 59
Henry's Demise: The Ultimate Breadhead 61
Mick's Mental Muck 65
Time to Take Us Back 67

Part Three

Sophomore's Send-off 71
Burning Baggage 73
Put Flowers on My Grave (Father to Son) 75
New Day, New Way 77
Mercia 79
Mary Kay's Wesley 87
Breadheads Remember Ben 89
Candi: Memories from the Islanders 91
Acknowledgments 93
About the Author 95
Thanks for reading! 96

Author's Note

THERE'S SOMETHING I WANT READERS to know about me before they dive into this collection: I'm a collector—not just of poems, but of people. Specifically, I collect groups of friends, each one bringing its own richness to my life. I'm passionate about nurturing these relationships. My husband, Eric, and I have built a life full of meaningful connections. Many of the poems are inspired by a few of the remarkable groups of friends that have deeply influenced me:

Normandy Gang: These are my first friends, my five siblings, and our childhood companions. We've shared countless adventures, and you'll meet them in "Weekend Fun." Despite the passing of time, we still come together to celebrate and support one another through life's ups and downs.

National Girls: I made these lifelong friends while working at National Supermarket in Riverview during my college years in the '80s. The setting in "Lucky Ladies" and "Work Snack" were written about this time. Jackie has been by my side ever since we met at National. She witnessed firsthand the stories of "Abby Rae's Birth" and "Jack's Birth." Sadly, I was not able to be by her side when she lost her husband to COVID. I wrote about her experience in "The Test of Time."

The Dream Group: A constant source of spiritual support, this group has guided me through life's challenges and opportunities. "Dream Retreat: A Bad Rap" offers a lighthearted take on one of our retreats gone awry.

The Islanders: When Eric and I first moved to Kirkwood, we found a close-knit community of neighbors who quickly became dear friends. We lived on a circular block we affectionately called "The Island," and together with eight other families, we formed the Islanders. Whether it was sitting around a fire, helping each other with projects, or simply chatting over the fence, these neighbors became a vital part of our lives. Even though some of us have since moved away, we remain connected. I wrote a poem for our beloved neightbor, Candi, when she passed away called, "Candi: Memories from the Islanders."

The Breadheads: We met while working at a bakery in downtown Kirkwood, and though none of us work there anymore, we still gather for dinners, sunsets, celebrations, and artist retreats. We're a collection of potters, painters, writers, and gardeners—each contributing beauty and creativity to the world around us. The poems "Burning Baggage," "Breadheads Remember Ben," and "Mick's Mental Muck" were written with this group in mind. A special thanks goes to Susan Zimmerman, Breadhead, potter, photographer, writer, editor, and creative cohort whose editing and handholding made this book possible.

These friendships have not only inspired my writing but have also helped shape the person I am today. As you read through these poems, I hope you feel the warmth and strength of the communities that have touched my heart.

PART ONE

*Mom and siblings in the 1970s (clockwise):
Jerry Jr., me (Kelly), Kath, Kay, Kris, Karen.*

Tom's Gone

I stared at my text
as the words sank in,
Tom *died this morning.*
I knew it was near.
He was riddled with cancer
the day we met.

I was the one assigned to take
him to the oncologist.
Tom's shortness of breath
and heart palpitations
raised concern,
his doctor sent us
to the emergency room STAT.

I wheeled Tom through the ER.
After signing in,
I spied a vacant seat
and slid his wheelchair next to me.
Tom protested that I need not stay,
but feeling protective
of this eighty-year-old man, I insisted.
Our conversation turned
to commonalities.
We both enjoyed
writing poetry,
both retired educators,

and care partners
for a loved one with Alzheimer's,
each recently passed.
His wife gone one year,
my special client gone three.
Five hours later, Tom's heart
was judged well enough
to go home, and mine
was changed forever.

Over the next year,
I visited Tom
as often as I could.
I would bring a poem
for him to critique,
or a video project
to narrate,
or my grandson
to entertain.

We walked when
his body allowed,
first to his condo's
courtyard where we sat
and shared poems.
As his endurance increased,
we took strolls to the corner
ice cream shop, indulging
in his favorite treat.
When he was stronger,

we drove to Forest Park
with my grandson
in tow to have lunch
at the Boat House
and feed the ducks.
Another time I took him
to visit my family's property
that sits on the Illinois bluffs
overlooking the small town of Columbia.
Our outings always
seemed to spark creative projects.

When he stopped his treatment,
the cancer spread
from his prostate
to other areas of his body.
Dying artfully became
his final project.

Tom arranged for a care team
to assist with meds and meals.
He planned his own green burial,
as he had for his wife.
When Tom became bedridden,
his neighbor friend stepped in
to oversee his care.
His nephew was assigned executor
of his estate and carried out
Tom's dying wishes.
At the end, friends and family

were with him when he passed
peacefully at home.
Tom was dearly loved
by all who knew him.

I look at the text again.
Tom died *this morning.*
My heart fills with regret.
I wish for a redo.
If granted,
I would complete
my poetry collection,
finish our video,
be more involved
in Tom's dying.
I wish for one more day
to tell him how special
he was to me.
I wouldn't change the subject
when he talked about dying.
I thought I was being
brave for him.
I had mistaken bravery
for denial. I should
have been a better listener.
I should have been there.
My morning smoothie
sits untouched,
yoga class goes

on without me.
I cannot muster up
one cleansing breath.

Tom died this morning.
I say the words out loud,
trying to convince myself
he's gone.
I can no longer show
him a poem
or share an idea.
I cannot thank him
for our time together.
I don't know what to do.
Tom would tell me to write.

So, I write.
I want the world to stop
for one lousy day,
this lousy day!
I want to nurse my sadness,
pierce my numbness,
allow myself time to be still.
I want to toast Tom's memory
with a shot of his Maker's Mark,
or indulge in a scoop of ice cream,
anything to feel connected to him today.

But life doesn't stop for death.
So, I pull myself together,
hurry up,
show up,
and try to be the person
Tom saw in me.

Daddy's Hand

I never appreciated when
Daddy held my hand.
I never relaxed long enough
to enjoy the awkward touch.
Too worried about when
he would let go.
I'd try to think of ways
to keep his grip in mine,
feeling foolish
for wanting his affection.
Take it easy,
go unnoticed,
for the slightest movement,
the moment would be gone.
Hold my hand longer,
I'd wish, but he never did.
He let go too soon,
and our touch slipped away.
Where did I go wrong?
My grip too insignificant?
I wanted his too long?
It would be a while
before Daddy's hand
returned back in mine.
In a way I was relieved,
too much pressure
for a kid my age.

Weekend Fun

AND IF I SPEAK of fond childhood memories, then I am speaking of the weekends.

In the seventies, my family home was the favorite place to be on the weekends, thanks to Mom. She taught eighth grade at St. Angela Merici while raising her six children, a boy and five girls. Her friends affectionately thought of Mom as the Pied Piper because kids loved being around her. And she loved being around them.

Mom looked forward to the weekends as much as her children. She didn't get uptight about the messes we'd make or the amount of friends we'd have over or the food we'd consume. All were welcome.

Mom didn't care that our beds were unmade, our rooms were unkept, or the floors unswept before friends arrived. Eventually the house would be picked up, but not on the weekends. Mom just didn't put much energy into tidiness. Other parents had a different opinion. They judged our lifestyle, not in a cool way like our friends, but more of a "*What kind of household are they running?*" way. True, it was chaotic, but it didn't change the way my parents functioned.

Friday night was our grab-the-popcorn, pour-the-soda TV night. My siblings and I had a friend (or two) spend the night. So instead of six of us, Mom usually had twelve or more mouths to feed. In the '70s, there were no VCRs, DVRs, or DVDs. No cable, internet, or streaming services. There were only four local stations. ABC aired the Friday night lineup of our favorite shows: *The Brady Bunch, Partridge Family, Room 222, The Odd Couple,* and *Love, American Style.*

Before the eight o'clock start, it was important to stake out a spot, for there was no moving or talking once the show began. Commercials were the only intermissions, that was our time to move around, make noise, and reload plates.

The weekend prep started after school on Friday. Mom took a couple of us with her to Kroger to buy the goods. We filled the cart with our favorites: popsicles, O-Ke-Doke cheese popcorn, cans of Vess soda, Twinkies, Ding Dongs, and Suzy Q's. We topped it off with our standard dinner, St. John's 10" individual frozen pizzas that came in multipacks of various toppings.

Before showtime, we started putting pizzas in the oven and setting out snacks. With paper plates piled high, we filed into the family room to crowd around our only television, a Zenith Color Console TV, equipped with bunny-ear antennae that sat on top. The person closest to the TV acted as the human remote—adjusting the volume, changing channels, or moving the tinfoil wrapped around the antennae for better reception. Mom always had the spot on the left end of the couch, next to the end table, so she had a place to grade papers. Sometimes she allowed us to grade spelling tests. Holding a red pen and putting a big red X on a misspelled word felt powerful and fun. Our friends loved the extra entertainment.

When *The Brady Bunch* started, we all sang along: "Here's a story of a lovely lady…"

If Friday night was TV night, Saturday was our parents' night out, leaving the "Little Ones"—Kath, Kris, and Kay (ten, nine, and six)—under the supervision of the "Big Ones"—Jerry, Karen, and myself (thirteen, twelve, eleven). Really, this meant the burden of babysitting was on Karen. We always had a houseful of overnight guests, some of whom never left from Friday night. The Little Ones played school in the basement or played games in their shared upstairs bedroom. Jerry and his friends would hang out in his room decorated with blacklight posters, listening to *The Beatles* album purchased at Peaches Record Store in Ferguson.

My best friend Mary Kay and I headed to the living room to play our 45s on the turntable in the credenza, making up dances or spying on my brother. Karen usually watched TV with her bestie, Alicia. My mother didn't have many rules for us to follow but one. If you spent the night on Saturday, you had to wake up and go to church on Sunday. Being a devout Catholic, this was the one rule she was willing to put her energy into, which meant that most friends went home at the end of the night.

Like a page out of *The Cat in the Hat*, our fun came to an abrupt end with a phone call from Mom informing us that she and Dad were coming home with friends in an hour. Karen usually answered our only phone that hung in the hallway. The long stretched-out cord attached to the receiver kept her anchored there until she got off the phone, then she sounded the alarm: *Adults! Adults are on their way! It's go time!*

Everyone stopped what they were doing; it was all-hands-on-deck! Karen and Alicia took charge of the family room, picking up shoes, clothes, pillows, covers, dishes, and throwing away empty cans of soda and wrappers left from the night before. The things that needed to go upstairs were thrown on the landing for Kris and Kay to sort through and run them to the owners' bedrooms. Kathleen and her friend picked up the living room and took out the vacuum to run on the carpet.

Mary Kay and I handled the kitchen. She cleaned with the most efficiency. Her weekly chores from her mother's training made her the perfect kid to handle the tough jobs. She never panicked and knew how to work quickly, giving orders to anyone standing around. I was given the job to clear the kitchen table, first putting away boxes of cereal and Nestle Quick, throwing away wrappers, trash, crumbs, and handing dirty glasses, bowls, and plates to Mary Kay. After she loaded and started the dishwasher, we both wiped down counters. Jerry took out the trash.

To make our power hour a little more exciting, we pretended that our parents' friends were evil villains who threatened to lock us in the dungeon if they found our home dirty, all the while laughing and carrying on as we raced to pick up a weekend's worth of fun.

Mom and Dad came home, sometimes with friends and sometimes not. Most of the time it was a ploy to get us to pick up before they got back. We didn't mind. Secretly we enjoyed their approval when they came home to a clean house.

Come Sunday morning, the weekend fun was over. It was the "get-up-get-dressed-NO-you-can't-sleep-in-YES-your-friend-has-to-go-to-church-NO-you-can-not-eat-before-mass-You-better-be-in-the-station-wagon-before-Dad-starts-the-car" morning madness. Once inside St. Ann's church, Mom could relax and be prayerful…until one of us got the giggles.

Chewing Gum and Duct Tape

You left me
in this broken home,
overwhelmed and all alone,
with bills to pay
and a mortgage to make,
holding it together
with chewing gum
and duct tape.

Thought you were
my soulmate,
guess that's
not our fate,
those dreams of mine
will have to wait.
Still hold a vision
for a good life
but won't have it
being your wife.

Getting buried
under life's debris,
two jobs and parenting
zap all my energy
while waiting for you
to come back to me,
holding it together
just barely.
Start the rumor drama,
I'll be the baby mama
if that's the way you want it.

Use the excuse,
made another mistake,
while I hold it together
with chewing gum
and duct tape.

Let your friend, Sharone,
pay for your phone
now that you're
part of her family plan.
Come get your clothes
but leave Gram's afghan.
Take the mosaic
we were making,
no patience
left for the life
we were shaping.
I'm done with this
gum sticking
and duct taping.

Your neglect
no longer ignored.
I am tired

and underinsured.
You should be the one
disgraced
by promises you've
escaped.
You don't have a clue.
I've been the one
holding it together for you!
It's time you find
your own damn glue.

Lindsey's Birth

Here is the story map
given in a birthday rap.
My belly was tight,
woke up in fright,
turned to my husband,
his stopwatch was summoned.
My contractions we clocked
before he called the doc.
They were minutes apart and strong,
but that didn't last long.
When they told us to wait,
I thought, *Wrong*.
We grabbed my bags
and Cody the dog,
dropped him off
with Ma and Pa,
then headed to St. Mary's.
Recollection of the ride varies,
all the jerky stops and swerves
were getting on my frazzled nerves.
Thankfully arrived in one piece,
contractions started to increase.
Lindsey's dad was a great labor coach,
focusing on my breath was our approach.
Labor was intense and draining
from all the pushing and straining.

Four hours later, she came out.
It's a girl! I heard the doctor shout.
First handed to her dad to cut the cord,
a healthy eight-pounder, thank the Lord!

As the first granddaughter,
she was spoiled rotten.
Lindsey's birthday story
will never be forgotten.
Told every second day of May
to her dismay,
but what can I say?
I'm her mother!

Lucky Ladies

Lucky makes his Saturday rounds, stopping to visit his two favorite ladies. First he picks up a few groceries at National Supermarket. The clerk at the customer service counter smiles when Lucky steps into her line. When it's his turn, Lucky asks about her daughter; she shares a funny toddler story. He hands her two dollars in exchange for two scratch-offs. The clerk tears off two *Lucky Sevens* from the roll of tickets. Lucky puts one in each hand and has her pick. She takes the one in his left. He leaves with the one in his right, wishes her luck, and waves goodbye.

Lucky walks next door to Baskin Robbins to visit his other favorite lady. The server greets him warmly. He orders his usual. She bags up a quart of chocolate mint. He pays and has her keep the change. He asks about her college classes, and she complains about the stress. Lucky hands her the remaining lottery ticket, wishes her luck, and waves goodbye.

When he returns home from his Saturday rounds, Lucky puts away the groceries, warms up last night's soup, and tells his wife about his day. He does not mention the lottery tickets; money has been tight since her stroke.

Lucky sits down next to his wife's recliner, where she is staring at the television. He kisses her forehead; she smiles as a commercial jingle blares. He picks up the remote and turns the volume down, asking what she's watching. There is no reply. He tests the temperature of the soup before he begins to feed her.

That same evening, one of his favorite ladies scratches off a twenty-thousand-dollar winning ticket. She claims the money and quits her job. News of her good fortune is not shared with Lucky, nor is any gratitude or lottery winnings.

One of her coworkers shares the news with Lucky. He develops a distaste for ice cream. Lucky still makes his Saturday rounds, less one stop.

Work Snack

Before our dinner break,
pickles and chips we'd make,
sitting on the back counter to take
between customers.

Sandwich the pickle
between two chips.
Its taste and texture
tingles the lips.
A motivational bag of tricks
adding to our pleasure.

Krunchers chips are
the best we found,
with hot deli
pickles sliced round.
A delicious salty,
savory mound
lingering on the tongue.

Opening the chip bag,
nostalgia takes flight
when pairing Krunchers
with the pickle bite.
Grocery store memories
come to light…
thirty-five years later.

Abby Rae's Birth

On a September
morning in 1994,
Abby's dad and I
walked out the door,
off to Christian Northwest
to induce my labor.
Two weeks past due date,
I was in favor.

Some say
that Abby Rae
should not have
made it that day.
Many babies
don't survive
a prolapsed cord,
the signs of it
our nurses ignored.
When HELP was roared
by my Momma Bear,
then the staff
started to care.
Once in the know
as her heart rate
dipped low,
reaction time quickened
to emergency mode.

Because the
umbilical cord
came out first,
every contraction
made breathing worse.
Into the OR we were herded,
a birthing tragedy diverted.
Born a healthy baby girl
who came to bless our world.
Lindsey waited fourteen years
for this day
to get her sister,
Abby Rae.

Forgotten Town

Taking in the view
from the Amtrak train
approaching next stop,
small-town Maine.

I see tread marks
in trailer parks,
discarded wood
where homes once stood,
lawns void of grass
and trash amassed,
a graveyard
of rusty cars,
a broken slide
and monkey bars.
Two young children
play in the dirt
next to a woman
hanging a shirt.

Crossing gate arms
lower over the street,
red lights flash
a quickened beat.
Warning bells
sound our arrival,
Train brakes squeal
then spit in idle.

Sitting on a bench
in a posture
of defense
a woman stares
at her phone
outside the local payday loan.
A liquor store's
neon lights
advertise Lucky Strikes,
Budweiser, Coors beer,
and "Lottery sold here."

Seven minutes
before departing,
a mother and child
begin boarding.
A man gets off
to light a smoke,
he is joined
by other folk.

The train stirs
upon the track,
smokers make
their way back.
A voice announces
the next stop.
I notice
as the train pulls out

a water tower adorned
with a smiley face
standing sadly
over this place.
Is it a witness to
a drug maker's greed?
Responsible for this
small-town bleed
of overdoses and
addiction cruelty?

If the tower could blare
its town's condition,
would Big Pharma care
or even listen?

Dream Walker

Why are you in my dreams
holding me so tight?
Something left unsaid
when I dumped you that night?

It's an evil thing to do,
making me dream of you,
taking over my sleep
and creating wild scenes,
showing up as a butterfly
and wrapping me in your wings,
then morphing into yourself
doing all kinds of naughty things.
Once you came as a conductor,
took my ticket and my clothes,
traveled the midnight train together,
exploring bodyscapes as roads.

Things would be better
if you just stayed away
cuz when I wake up,
I think of you all day.
A dream hangover,
an emotional bulldozer,
a what-if takes over.

Glad to be rid
of your unfaithful ways.
You were not worth
those long, painful days.
Better off without you,
there is no doubt,
I knew it back then
and know it now.

I have a good life
that is truly gratifying,
but sneak into my dreams
and there is no denying
you.

Jack's Birth

It was a magical time,
end of month nine.
Labor pains interrupted
our morning juice
and bacon.
We packed the car
and left for St. Mary's
in Clayton.

After walking the halls
and sitting on balls,
Jack's heartbeat turned weak.
Not another bad streak?
I can't take a repeat
like Abby's birth.
Luckily, good friend Lynn
was our nurse,
closely monitoring
in case things turned worse.

Circumstances were
not looking great,
The doctor was running late.
Baby in distress
could not wait.
They wheeled me
to the OR around eight.

C-section was the direction
until Doc arrived with his objection.
Baby sounded fine was his detection.
He left it up to me:
have a caesarean or naturally?

I opted for the VBAC*;
hours later, out came Jack.
My good-luck charm
snug in my arm.
A healthy boy weighing 8.3,
so happy he was born to me.

*VBAC is a vaginal birth after cesarean.

PART TWO

Henry as a puppy. Looks adorable, but wasn't.

The D-Word

It snaked through my heart
as our detachment set in.
I ignored its presence
until I could no longer.

I struggled to find the right time to talk,
a time when it wouldn't ruin
a good mood or a night's sleep,
or turn a bad day worse.
When anger arose,
the words escaped my mouth,
not the ones
I had rehearsed, but a litany
of grievances randomly spewed out,
ending with the D-word,
a sound that rattled us both.

Marriage therapy, coexisting,
and finally, came the uncoupling.
Telling the kids was the most difficult.
What does a mother say
to her nine and four-year-old?

I intended to tell them
one night at McDonald's
after Happy Meals
and playing in "happy land,"
but I couldn't find the words.
Before leaving the parking lot,
I buckled them in
and broke the news.
It poisoned any kind of happy
they were feeling.

Everyone felt its constriction,
especially the children
as they were mandated
to split their time between houses.
Family and friends took sides.
Loyalties were lost and gained.
Over the years, its grip weakened.
New normals, traditions,
and stepfamilies were created.

Twenty-something years later,
the past is merely molted skin.
The children are young adults now
in charge of their own time,
their own lives, yet a faint trace
of venom still pulses.

Dream Retreat: A Bad Rap

Here's a story
in all its glory.
It was our dream retreat.
Take a seat, it ain't sweet.

In the evening,
we were just
chillin' 'n millin'
around the table,
thought we were stable
until Linda lit up a smoke,
suggested Rosie take a toke.
They coughed and choked,
laughed and joked,
when off her chair, Linda fell.
What the hell?
Heart attack?
She smoking smack?
"Are you okay?" I asked,
trying not to scream.
She replied, "Just having a dream."

What the shit?
Linda was out of it.
Stood her up,
another fall.
911 we had to call.

Best for all
to have medics
check her out.
Linda started to pout.
"Girl, I'm not playing around.
You can't get off the ground!"

Ambulance finally came.
Febreze hid the shame.
Blood pressure very low.
To the hospital she must go.

Took her away on a gurney.
Thus started the journey.
I followed in the rain.
So insane!
Must refrain
from feeling a scare.
Made it to St. Claire,
found Linda in Room 8
with an IV to hydrate.

When her condition was evaluated,
Linda reiterated
the scene that
some participated.
I didn't want to be associated,
but her recall incriminated.
Linda, please,
leave out the WE!
Geez.

"What kind of retreats
do you girls hold?"
the doc asked all judgy,
arms in a fold.
The magic of our dreams
fell on deaf ears,
but this incident will be told
by us for years.
It goes down as one
of our retreats' brightest,
belly-laughing,
tear-producing finest.
Thanks to Linda for the moment
and *her* illegal component.

Third Time's a Charm: An Anniversary Poem

Thanks for being such
a light in my world
and shining it bright
on this old girl.
You've a great mind,
one of a kind,
an I-N-F-P
just like me!
Smart with money,
kind of funny,
intriguing,
always believing
in the power of WE.
You're my gravity,
my sanity,
my happily
ever afterly.

We met at Sunday school
where the kids deemed you cool.
Unity teacher and single dad,
the kind of mentor I wanted to have.
We had playdates with our children.
You were my one in a million.
Our friendship enhanced,
grew into a romance.
We both gave marriage
another chance.

As husband and wife,
we made a good life.
Blended our families
as best we could,
bought a house
in the burbs of Kirkwood.

Now that the kids are all grown,
you and I have playdates of our own.
Still love you to the core.
Cheers to our years and
many more.

A Mother's Worry

I pick up my phone.
You coming home?
It's 12:10.
Late again.
Sleep disturbed.
I'm perturbed.
Some of us work, you jerk!
I'm sounding like a bitch,
but fear you're lying in a ditch.
Oh, brother!
Sound like my mother.
Drifting in and out of sleep,
I wake for a time-check peek.
Now it's one.
You're so done.
I need slumber.
I call your number.
You don't pick up.
I sit up.
With my thumbs
I yell like hell,
    C-A-L-L (send)
    M-E (send)
    N-O-W (send)
    Y-O-U-N-G (send)
    M-A-N (send)

My texting fit
goes on a bit.
You little shit!
I'll take your phone away…
as soon as you come home okay.
I can't sleep
or count sheep.
I picture you needing me.
Fear is feeding me.
This worry isn't fair.
I think I'm losing hair.

At 1:09
you send a line,
I'M FINE.
No need to shout.
Didn't go out.
Turned off my ringer.
Did you ever consider
to check my bed
instead,
the text read.

I turn off the light
and text, Goodnight.

Mundane Moments

I like time measured
in milestones.
Weddings are good time holders,
hair appointments are not.
It's the day-to-day moments
that are hard to reconcile.

I examine the top
of my head in the mirror
where the gray streak
grows along the part.
It was my niece's wedding day
when I last had my hair done.
I wore it up in a loose bun
with pearl earrings
that complemented
my sparkly dress.
Such a nice occasion.
Has it been eight weeks
since I last dyed my hair?

When I squeeze the last drop
of toothpaste
from the flattened tube
and try to account for my time
between brushings,

when my to-do list
goes unchecked
and keeps getting longer,
I feel the days slipping by.

When the last few
bits of dog food expose
an empty container,
when the milk
expires before I finish
my box of Cheerios,
when the dirty laundry
fills the hamper
I just emptied,
these mundane moments
get the best of me.
Can dogs eat Cheerios?

Milestones are my markers.
I can take stock of life
with family vacations,
celebrations, anniversaries,
weddings, except funerals.
Death disrupts time,
shakes it off-kilter,
moving slowly
and quickly all at once.

Funerals blur my markers.
I cannot remember
who was there,
what was said,
what I wore,
or how I got
through it
without you.

The Test of Time

Mornings when Jackie wakes up
and does *not* smell the coffee,
or evenings when she comes home
to an empty house, she feels his absence.

Guilt-ridden memories
keep her up at night
and replay until slumber
comes to her rescue.
Alone, dying in the hospital,
Pete struggles to breathe
while a nurse
in a hazmat suit
holds a phone to his face,
connecting them
with FaceTime.

Alone, quarantined at home,
Jackie struggles to breathe
between sobs while
watching her husband die
on the small screen.
Is this the end?
Will she be able
to endure it?

They lose connection.
She is left holding her phone
wondering why.
She makes no attempt
to call back.

This is not the ending that
Jackie imagined.
She was preparing herself
to be Pete's caregiver
through his last stage
of lung cancer.
When the time came,
she would be the one
to take care of him,
be the strong one
for a change,
make up for the mistakes
in their fifty years of marriage.
She would be the one
holding his hand surrounded
by family and friends
as he took his final breath.
COVID robbed her
of that ending.
Jackie sobs and curses
the virus. Pete. God.
Why did Pete choose
to stay off a ventilator?
Why is this happening?

The day of his funeral
is the first time she's
able to touch Pete
since he was admitted
into the hospital.
She stays close
to the casket.
Only Jackie
and her immediate family
are allowed to attend,
masked and sitting
six feet apart.
The absence
of human touch
fuels her grief.

Afterwards, friends and
extended family parade
by the house to express
condolences from their cars
while Jackie, her son and
daughter, their spouses,
and three grandchildren
sit in lawn chairs
on the driveway
to receive them.

Years have come and gone.
The pandemic is over
yet the virus still lingers.
Granddaughters are
in college now.
A new grandson
fills her time.
Jackie learns to walk
in a world without Pete.

Time heals, they say.
She finds this
to be true
except the guilt.
Guilt does not fade.
It stands
the test of time.

Pop

Across the ocean,
terrorism rages
at our borders,
children locked in cages,
in the hood,
a shooting enrages.
World in disrepair,
I try not to despair,
losing all hope,
need medication to cope.
Worry floods my head,
can't get out of bed,
can't sleep,
want to weep.
A cult of hocus-pocus
to change democracy
as we know it,
fake news as Trump sows it.
How to keep my focus?
Ignore the news,
pretend that I'm immune
to the actions of this buffoon,
his cronies, and tycoons?
Live in my fantasy cocoon,
all rainbows and balloons…
until it pops?

Henry's Demise: The Ultimate Breadhead

When old Duke died,
it was his time,
but Henry dying
felt like a crime.

The dog sitter
found him dead
trying to eat
a loaf of bread.
It must have
been dramatic
to find his head
stuck in plastic.

Those who knew Henry
were not surprised
to hear that food
was his demise.
He was the
"break-up puppy"
that Abby brought home
to make her happy.
Alas, her pup-wish
with a food fetish
had an insatiable hunger
that tragically took him under.

Abby turned
such a sad girl
when a boy
crushed her world,
that's why we agreed
in her time of need
to this Beagle breed.
When a new semester
came around,
she went back
to college town,
leaving us
with a whiny hound.
Henry was more
of a pain than a mate,
like the times
he got out of the gate
left open by mistake.
We lured him back
with treats as bait.
When the kibbles rattled,
he'd stop to check,
then we'd quickly put
a leash around his neck.

Our old dog, Duke, taught
Henry a few tricks,
how to use the doggy door,
shake a paw for chips.
Duke had to be put down
when his old body got sick.

Henry did not stay
the only pet source;
he was joined by
another furry force.
A Schnoodle puppy,
named Bentley,
that eased his way
in gently.

When we found ourselves
singing the *empty-nest* song,
we downsized to a condo,
and the dogs came along.
Some of our new neighbors
wanted Henry gone.
He violated the bylaw,
"ONE SMALL dog per lawn."
It took a lawyer's fee,
votes of the HOA majority,
to change the law
and keep Henry in the family.

Memories of Henry's antics
make me smile.
Like when Eric played guitar,
and Henry would howl;
taking walks
on a hot day,
he'd plop down
in the shade
refusing to obey.

When doors left ajar,
he'd enter a neighbor's home,
sniffing out food, toys,
or an unattended bone.
After getting notification
of Henry's location,
we usually found
our hound
dropped off
at the fire station.

I am not making
up this stuff;
he seriously made
our lives tough!
And if that's not enough,
missing him has been
really…ruff.

Mick's Mental Muck

When Mick's darkness
shadows day into night,
he needs a reflection
that mirrors his light.
Depression crushes
down like elephants,
making Mick blind
to his benevolence.
He misses the evidence
of his intelligence;
he doesn't see
his goodness
or his kindness
when gloom blindness
leaves him motionless.

Depression doesn't
define his talented mind.
He has a chill essence,
a peaceful presence.
Lest we not forget
his hamburger savviness,
connoisseur of the beef pattiness.

His self-talk harassment,
emotional detachment
gets him stuck
in mental muck.
Depression turbulence
can feel like permanence,
but things do change,
thoughts rearrange.

Let him turn up the sad song,
dance and sing along.
Movement is medicine,
a one-step regiment.
It feels good
to feel sadness
to help get out
of blandness.
No need to fix it,
no need to advise,
just sit with Mick
and empathize.
When darkness
shadows day into night,
be the reflection
that mirrors his light.

Time to Take Us Back

I wish I was your guitar
hanging on the wall.
If time, you'd play me
in a fancy concert hall.
I'd make the sounds
as you'd strum my strings.
Together we'd harmonize,
dance, and sing.

We'd be one
in this world again,
creating a sensation,
earning a standing ovation
from fan adoration.

But no time to play,
no time to slack.
Got to make a living,
time to put me back.

I wish I was your tractor
parked in the shed.
If time, you'd ride me
through the fields ahead.
Straddle my frame
and grip the wheel.
Rev my engine
and off we'd peal.

We'd be one in
this world again,
sharing the vibration,
stopping at the gas station,
feeling the tractor admiration.

But no time to play,
no time to slack.
Got to make a living,
time to put me back.

I wish I was a bunch of grapes
ripening on the vine.
When ready, you'd harvest
and turn me into wine.
I'd bring a taste of heaven
and satisfy your thirst.
You'd put me in your mouth
and feel my flavors burst.

We'd be one
in this world again,
giving into temptation,
sharing the libation,
rewriting our narration.

It's time to play,
and time to slack.
Got to start living,
it's time to take us back.

PART THREE

Sketch of lawn ornament on our farm by Hannah Battista.

Sophomore's Send-off

You loaded your car with all your stuff,
gave me a hug, and left in a huff.
Send you money and you'll be fine,
tuition bill can be paid online.

You'll pay me back for the credits missed,
do your homework, and follow the syllabus.
This year will be different than last,
not an option to fail, you need to pass.

Promise me that you'll try harder,
show up for class,
put your best foot forward.
Get out of bed when doldrums
fog your head.
There is no debate
to skip class or show up late.

Freedom and responsibility
go hand in hand;
when you put forth the effort,
you'll understand.
You're getting a job at night?
Please tell me I heard that right!

There's so much you don't know
that I could teach before you go.
But when I try to advise,
you just roll your eyes.
Do you know abut the dryer?
How the lint trap can cause fire?

Old habits are hard to change.
Time to put expectations in range.
Empty promises are like broken ladders;
it's the climb that really matters.

Burning Baggage

Sitting around the fire
with the past,
letters from lovers
who didn't last,
old journals
and diaries stacked,
feeding them to the flames.
Burning changes energy,
fuels the power
of our synergy.

Family eyes
will not find
the memories
confined
in these boxes,
words that
once defined us,
past ties
that no longer bind us.

Burn, baby, burn.
No more guilt
or regret,
need to move on,
forget.

Time for selfish solitude,
to build an artist attitude.
Let this burning
inspire a yearning
to create our next act.
Don't be cast
as a washed-up bella.
Never settle for the role
of Cinder-fucking-rella.

Put Flowers on My Grave (Father to Son)

Put flowers on my grave
if that helps you remember me,
but know I am always with you
when caring for my legacy.

I am connected to you
in the fields you mow,
the seeds you sow,
the harvest you reap,
the family you keep.
I am the energy on the bluff,
my corny jokes you used to snuff,
which now you can't tell enough.
Visit the cemetery if you must.

I'd rather you take time
to sit on the hill,
soaking in the goodwill,
this place of your birth,
and my death here on earth.
Feel the brush of my hand
in the breeze on the land.

If you put flowers on my grave,
do it for you, not me.
My spirit's part of you now
and both our legacies.

New Day, New Way

I went to bed early,
after two glasses of wine.
When I finally woke up,
it was 7:49!
Did I not set the alarm clock?
Did I turn off the snooze?
Now scrambling to get dressed
and swearing off the booze.
I wanted a leisurely morning,
so I didn't have to rush,
but no time to stretch,
eat, or give teeth a brush.
The list to get ready
I raced to check.
The stress of it all
knotting up my neck.

I tripped over the dog
heading out to work.
I slammed the door shut,
feeling like a jerk.
I checked my calendar,
noting the time.
I turned back to pet that
furry friend of mine.

As I was thinking about how
my morning backfired,
it dawned on me that
last week I retired.
With a heavy sigh,
I picked up Freddy.
Time for us to go
back to beddy.

Mercia

You would not have known
that you were her only
emergency contact.
You had not
spoken to Mercia
in over two years.
She was
embarrassed
by her ugly boyfriend
who had a history
of domestic violence.

Not many knew,
but you did,
that Mercia lived
with an ache
in her heart,
an emptiness that
neither her adoptive parents,
friends, lovers,
nor alcohol
could ever fill.
That emptiness eventually
landed her at the bottom
of a dark canyon of grief.

The destructiveness
of her drinking
became harder
for you to witness.
She went from one
toxic relationship
to the next.
And then became
involved with the ugly boyfriend.
He was her neighbor.
"Don't date your neighbor,
Mercia."
"Do not move in with him,"
you warned.
You pleaded.
She ignored.

She was spiraling
out of control,
and control her
you could NOT.
But he could.
He could make her
feel special;
convince her
to move in
with him;
make her stop
communicating with you.

After two years
you still worried
about Mercia.
You occasionally searched
social media.
An unsettling feeling
arose in your gut
every time you
could not find her.
You were not able
to search his name
because she
never told you.

And then,
one day,
after your last search,
you got the call.
You knew she was dead
before the detective
uttered the words.
He spared the details,
only categorizing it
as a violent death.

You learned more
details after reading
an article about
a domestic murder-suicide.

It reported that
two bodies were found
after a tenant complained
about the growing stench
in the apartment hallway
where Mercia
and her murderer lived.

You called her brother,
her only living
family member.
He had not spoken
to his sister
in over twenty years.
He was grateful
you reached out.
You filled him in
about the last part
of her life,
as much as you
knew anyway.
You both cried.
You promised
to keep in touch;
help him with
his sister's
Celebration of Life,
whatever he needed.
You wanted
to honor Mercia
and the friendship

you had;
celebrate her life
with the others
who loved Mercia;
let it be known that
her life mattered.

When you went
to sleep that night,
you showed up
at her apartment
and found yourself
in her closet.
From the darkness,
you heard
television noises,
then yelling,
name calling,
a gun shot,
an eerie silence
accompanied
by television sounds,
another gunshot.

When courage
found its way
to your extremities,
you opened
the bedroom door.
You saw Mercia
lying on the couch,

his lifeless body
on the floor.
Blood covered
the violence.
She turned to you
and smiled
as if she knew
you were with her
all this time.
"No more, my friend.
I'm out of here,"
she said.
You reached for her hand
to help her up.
Her bloody arm turned
into a wing
and her body morphed
into a raven
as she flew
through the window.

A scream woke you.
It was yours.
You sat up startled,
caught your breath,
and looked around the room
to get your bearings.
You exhaled a sigh of relief
and laid your head back
on your pillow.

"Free at last, Mercia.
Rest in peace. Finally,"
you whispered.
A gentle breeze,
from the open window,
brushed your wet cheek.

Mary Kay's Wesley

He was his
mother's charmer,
a real heart-warmer.
There was a time
when he and she
were close;
she misses
that the most.

He played football
as a little squirt,
grew to be
a handsome flirt.
His prowess in soccer
and his great skill
made watching from
the sidelines
a true thrill.
Asked to be on
a traveling team,
but circumstances
kept him from
that dream.
He made bad choices,
his mother knows.
It wasn't till later
that his addiction showed.

Had a way about him,
charismatic and sweet.
Left behind a daughter,
a son he would never meet.
He was a wonderful father
and a good guy when clean.
The thought of him gone
makes her blood boil mean.

The anger that festers,
Mary Kay won't succumb;
better to feel the loss
rather than live numb.
Wesley and his mother
share the same heart.
One physically gone
but never apart.

Breadheads Remember Ben

We met Ben in Elsah
standing on a rooftop,
came down to greet us
and offered us a cold pop.
His handsome smile
with cowboy flare,
so dang cute
and unaware
the cause of Lynn's gray hair.
You knew right away
he was one of a kind;
scolded by his daughter,
he paid her no mind,
continued to climb
into his decade of nine.

Acts of kindness
were his game,
saving a deer
brought him fame.
Against the mayor's advice,
Ben walked out
on the river ice
to calm the doe
who fell through.
He kept her safe
until in flew
animal rescue.

Mayor's dad got lots of views
when caught on the local news.

A New Yorker with a fearless gene,
joined the Navy at age fifteen,
raised a family in Illinois,
two daughters and a boy.
Despite a difficult wife,
he lived an authentic life.

His legacy lives on
in his accordion songs,
the stone walls
around Lynn's lawns,
master knots passed on
from his Navy days
to grandson's knots
now praised,
and a granddaughter's
owl-loving craze.

May Ben's many lessons
be part of our blessings.

Candi: Memories from the Islanders

When Mark got a job
in the Lou,
Candi said goodbye
to her LA crew.
She brought her West Coast style
and her sunshine smile.

So began her tour of duty
as a fresh Midwest newbie.
First time the tornado siren sounded,
a bike helmet upon her head was mounted
while she stood in a doorway frame
as if in an earthquake pregame.
When Candi first came to
the neighborhood jam circle
without a rehearsal,
she took Eric's six-string,
started to strum,
and began to sing
Leaving on a Jet Plane.
"Dang! Pop the champagne!
She's good," proclaimed Jane.

Candi could have snubbed us
or the wrong way rubbed us;
instead, she became one of us.
A village of "Island Aunties"
now infused with the energy of Candi's.

A fun party host,
didn't like to boast
that she was better
at ping-pong than most,
although Mark's skills
were close.

Dealing with kids in adolescence,
Candi volunteered her presence.
She often listened with empathy,
didn't judge or try to remedy.
Once our neighbor had
to drop off her daughter far away;
Candi rode along in their car that day
so her friend didn't have
to feel so alone
when driving home.

Looking out for others' needs,
making her killer grilled cheese,
growing her own strawberries.
How lucky are we
to have such
fond memories!

Acknowledgments

FIRST AND FOREMOST, my heartfelt thanks to my editor, Susan Zimmerman. Without her unwavering support and patience, this book would not have made it to print. Our editing sessions were a gift of magical collaboration and countless cups of coffee. I am deeply grateful for her gentle critiques during my many revisions, her masterful polishing techniques, and her efforts to keep me on track.

I extend my gratitude to Peggy Nehmen at N-K Creative for her professional expertise, book design, and invaluable resources that contributed to the success of this project.

A special thank you to Hannah Battista for her work on the cover design and photo sketch.

To Robyn Keough who keeps me out of the mental muck. Thanks for your encouragement and faith in me.

I am also deeply thankful to my family and friends for their appreciation of my poems over the years. They provide great material.

Last but certainly not least, my deepest gratitude goes to my husband, Eric. He has been my biggest fan and greatest supporter. Thanks for putting up with my creative mind.

About the Author

KELLY CARTER SCHNEIDER IS a native St. Louisan and a member of the Academy of American Poets. After twenty years as an elementary school teacher, she shifted her focus to working as a care partner for seniors. She now devotes her time to writing, family, and travel. *Time to Take Us Back* is her debut poetry book.

Schneider and her husband spend time between their home in Kirkwood, Missouri and their barndominium in Columbia, Illinois. She enjoys good trouble and good company which includes visits with her kids and grandchildren who live throughout the Midwest.

Thanks for reading!

I'D LOVE TO HEAR from you.
Please leave a review or visit my website at
KellySchneiderWrites.com for book events,
upcoming projects, or to hear what others are saying.